THE LEARNING ELEPHANT™

This book is for my parents, Shing and Angela.
They left Myanmar to start a new life in America for me
and my sister. Our parents instilled strong work ethics,
taught us to do things honestly, and to never give up.

Thank you for being our role models.

DEAR PARENTS

All information can be found on the American Academy of Pediatric Dentistry Website (www.aapd.org). Please remember every child is unique in their appearance, growth, and personality. On the following pages you will see there is a blank line next to each lettered tooth. This is so you can put the date of when each tooth erupts in your child's mouth. If you are not able to…it is totally okay. This book is meant to be fun and entertaining for your little one. We hope this will be a book you and your child can treasure for a lifetime! Sam and I enjoyed our first book together, and we look forward to many more in the future!

······· This book belongs to: ·······

_____

······· Date of the first dental visit: ·······

_____

······· Name of my Pediatric Dentist: ·······

_____

······· City and State: ·······

_____

Charlotte and her twin brother Oli are eight years old. They love to read, travel, and learn about different jobs that grown-ups do. Come join them on their adventures and be a part of the fun!

What do YOU want to be when you grow up?

Charlotte
wants to be a...
Pediatric Dentist

An Interactive Children's Book

Written by Jessica Loo Marn, DDS.

Illustrated by Sarmite Lau

ISBN: 978-1-73517-322-1

1st edition (2020)
The Learning Elephant
128 Mott St., Suite 403
New York, N.Y 10013
Thelearningelephant2020@gmail.com

Ordering information: Please contact The Learning Elephant
Printed in the United States of America on SFI certified paper.

www. TheLearningElephant**.com**

of Me and My Dentist:

Primary "Baby" Teeth

UPPER TEETH	erupt	shed
central incisors	6-10 mos.	7-8 yrs.
lateral incisors	8-12 mos.	8-9 yrs.
canines	16-20 mos.	11-12 yrs.
first molars	11-18 mos.	9-11 yrs.
second molars	20-30 mos.	9-12 yrs.

LOWER TEETH	erupt	shed
second molars	20-30 mos.	11-13 yrs.
first molars	11-18 mos.	10-12 yrs.
canines	16-20 mos.	9-11 yrs.
lateral incisors	7-10 mos.	7-8 yrs.
central incisors	5-8 mos.	6-7 yrs.

Hi everyone. My name is Charlotte, and this is my brother Oliver, and my puppy Hoku. You can call me Dr. Charlotte. I am training to become a pediatric dentist. I will take you on a tour of my room, which is also my dental office.

Can you find these items at your pediatric dentist's office?

Check the box as soon as you spot them!

- ☐ Receptionist
- ☐ Phones
- ☐ Computers
- ☐ Toys
- ☐ Books
- ☐ Dental Assistant
- ☐ Dental Chair
- ☐ Dental Light
- ☐ Eyewear Protectors
- ☐ Bib
- ☐ Masks
- ☐ Gloves
- ☐ Dentist

- ☐ X-ray Machine
- ☐ Explorer (Cavity Detector)
- ☐ Mirror
- ☐ Toothbrush
- ☐ Floss and Flosser
- ☐ Prizes

- ☐ What else did you find?

_____

_____

_____

Once you sit down in the dental chair, the dentist will count your teeth. It is just like at school when your teacher takes attendance. Every tooth has a birthday. I like to give them names and pretend characters. Come meet my characters!

Ellie the Elephant and Finn the Falcon
Appear between 6 - 10 months.

#E:_____   #F:_____

Pearl the Penguin and Oscar the Octopus
Appear between 5 - 8 months.

#P:_____   #O:_____

D   E   F   G

Daniel the Dinosaur and Grace the Giraffe
Appear between 8 - 12 months.

#D:_____   #G:_____

Quinn the Quail and Natalie the Narwhal
Appear between 7 - 10 months.

#Q:_____   #N:_____

Q   P   O   N

Bella the Butterfly and Ivan the Iguana
Appear between 11 - 18 months.

#B:_____   #I:_____

Sally the Seal and Leo the Lion
Appear between 11 - 18 months.

#S:_____   #L:_____

Catherine the Cat and Henry the Horse
Appear between 16 - 20 months.

#C:_____ #H:_____

Riley the Rabbit and Michael the Monkey
Appear between 16 - 20 months.

#R:_____ #M:_____

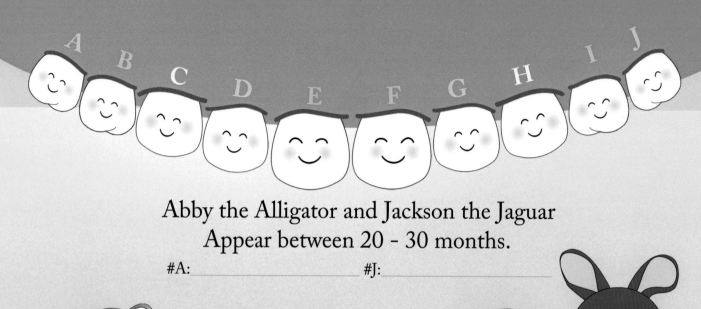

Abby the Alligator and Jackson the Jaguar
Appear between 20 - 30 months.

#A:_____   #J:_____

Tommy the Tiger and Katie the Kangaroo
Appear between 20 - 30 months.

#T:_____   #K:_____

Now that you know all the characters and names of your teeth, it is very important for you to take good care of them. Please brush your teeth twice a day for two minutes each time, with the help of an adult. Drink plenty of water, and eat fresh fruits and vegetables to keep your teeth nice and strong! Remember to see your pediatric dentist every six months for a cleaning and a check-up to keep your smile healthy.

Dr. Charlotte had a great time teaching you about your baby teeth. Keep smiling and we will see you again soon!

Do what you love and everything
else will fall into place.

xoxo. Jessica ☺

About the Author

My patients call me Dr. Jessica. I am a Board-Certified pediatric dentist practicing in N.Y.C. since 2001. This book was inspired by many years of practicing pediatric dentistry and the special bonds I made throughout the years with my patients and their families. The special bond attributes to the trust built between myself and my patients, the commitment of the parents to bring their children for routine dental cleanings and treatments, and my patients' understanding the importance of good oral hygiene and habits. I am extremely fortunate to have the opportunity to watch my patients grow from children to young adults. Thank you to my patients and future patients for allowing me to be a part of your journey.

Thank you also to Sam, the illustrator of this book, and mom of Marcus and Katherine, who I watched grow for the past 10 years. This book and the experiences would not be possible if it were not for the love, support, and encouragement of my husband, Rich, and our wonderful children, Samuel and Sophia.

About the Illustrator

Hi, my name is Sarmite Lau, but everybody calls me Sam. Originally from Latvia, I have lived in New York for over twenty years. After graduating from Riga Technical University, I found myself struggling in the field and looking for a different path for myself. It is only when I moved to New York and met my husband, Keng, that I was fortunate enough to discover the creative side of me. Keng taught me art. He taught me how to draw and how to look at things from a different perspective. I am a graphic designer, art director, a special events coordinator, and now a book illustrator who understands and embraces the juggling demands of wearing many different hats.

I am also a proud mom of two kids, Katherine and Marcus, who have become my inspiration and my motivation in life. Meeting and working with like-minded families like the Marn family and Dr. Jessica, in particular, was the best part of illustrating this book. Thank you for bringing me along in your journey, Dr. Jessica!

Sam ♡

Learn Your Alphabet!

A	B	C	D	E	F
G	H	I	J	K	L
M	N	O	P	Q	R
S	T	U	V	W	X
Y	Z

Learn Your Alphabet!

a	b	c	d	e	f
g	h	i	j	k	l
m	n	o	p	q	r
s	t	u	v	w	x
y	z				

Who is Your **FAVORITE**?